# RUSSIANS IN AMERICA

web enhanced at **www.inamericabooks.com**

ALISON BEHNKE

LERNER PUBLICATIONS COMPANY / MINNEAPOLIS

Current information and statistics quickly become out of date. That's why we developed **www.inamericabooks.com**, a companion website to the **In America** series. The site offers lots of additional information—downloadable photos and maps and up-to-date facts through links to additional websites. Each link has been carefully selected by researchers at Lerner Publishing Group and is regularly reviewed and updated. However, Lerner Publishing Group is not responsible for the accuracy or suitability of material on websites that are not maintained directly by us. It is recommended that students using the Internet be supervised by a parent, a librarian, a teacher, or another adult.

Lerner Publications Company
A division of Lerner Publishing Group
241 First Avenue North
Minneapolis, MN 55401 U.S.A.

Website address: www.lernerbooks.com

Library of Congress Cataloging-in-Publication Data

Behnke, Alison.
    Russians in America / by Alison Behnke.
       p.   cm. – (In America)
    Includes bibliographical references and index.
    ISBN-13: 978-0-8225-3954-4 (lib. bdg. : alk. paper)
    ISBN-10: 0-8225-3954-3 (lib. bdg. : alk. paper)
    1. Russian Americans—History—Juvenile literature. 2. Immigrants—United States—History—Juvenile literature. I. Title. II. Series: In America series.
    E184.R9B37 2006
    973'.049171–dc22
                                      2004014789

Manufactured in the United States of America
1  2  3  4  5  6 – JR – 11  10  09  08  07  06

# CONTENTS

INTRODUCTION . . . . . . . . . . . . . . . . . 4
*Russians in America*

1 • MOTHER RUSSIA . . . . . . . . . . . . . 6
*Old Country*
*An Empire Is Born*
*Russian Life*
*Fleeing for Faith*
*Beyond the Pale*
*The First Wave*

2 • BETWEEN TWO WORLDS . . . . . 22
*"He Who Doesn't Work, Doesn't Eat"*
*A Roof and a Stove*
*Feeling at Home*
*Revolution*

3 • WAVES OF CHANGE . . . . . . . . . 40
*Death of an Era*
*Seeing Red*
*Stalin's Refugees*
*Cold Shoulder*
*Looking Forward*

FAMOUS RUSSIAN AMERICANS . . . . . 62
TIMELINE . . . . . . . . . . . . . . . . . . . . . 68
GLOSSARY . . . . . . . . . . . . . . . . . . . . . 70
THINGS TO SEE AND DO . . . . . . . . . 71
SOURCE NOTES . . . . . . . . . . . . . . . . 72
SELECTED BIBLIOGRAPHY . . . . . . . . . 73
FURTHER READING & WEBSITES . . . 74
INDEX . . . . . . . . . . . . . . . . . . . . . 78

# INTRODUCTION

In America, a walk down a city street can seem like a walk through many lands. Grocery stores sell international foods. Shops offer products from around the world. People strolling past may speak foreign languages. This unique blend of cultures is the result of America's history as a nation of immigrants.

Native peoples have lived in North America for centuries. The next settlers were the Vikings. In about A.D. 1000, they sailed from Scandinavia to lands that would become Canada, Greenland, and Iceland. In 1492 the Italian navigator Christopher Columbus landed in the Americas, and more European explorers arrived during the 1500s. In the 1600s, British settlers formed colonies that, after the Revolutionary War (1775–1783), would become the United States. And in the mid-1800s, a great wave of immigration brought millions of new arrivals to the young country.

Immigrants have many different reasons for leaving home. They may leave to escape poverty, war, or harsh governments. They may want better living conditions for themselves and their children. Throughout its history, America has been known as a nation that offers many opportunities. For this reason, many immigrants come to America.

Moving to a new country is not easy. It can mean making a long, difficult journey. It means leaving home and starting over in an unfamiliar place. But it also means using skill, talent, and determination to build a new life. The In America series tells the story of immigration to the United States and the search for fresh beginnings in a new country—in America.

# RUSSIANS IN AMERICA

According to population estimates, anywhere from 3 to 5 million people of Russian descent live in the United States. This community came to America through four major waves of immigration. The first began in the late 1800s and stretched into the early 1900s, as Russians left their homeland to escape poverty, hardship, and injustice—especially in the form of religious persecution.

A second wave took place in the years following the Russian Revolution of 1917. In the midst of war and dramatic political upheaval, many people who disagreed with Russia's new government fled to other countries, including the United States. Another war sparked the next wave of Russian immigration, as World War II (1939–1945) created thousands of refugees from Russia, which by then was part of a group of nations called the Soviet Union. Ruled by the dictator Joseph Stalin, Russians and other Soviet citizens suffered political oppression, poverty, hunger, and fear.

The fourth wave of Russian immigration to the United States began as a trickle in the 1960s. In the following decades, more and more Soviets grew dissatisfied with government policies. Many risked their lives to escape. As time went on and the nation began to crumble, poverty and unrest forced others out. Then, amidst the chaos of the Soviet Union's collapse in 1991, that trickle grew to a flood. And in the 2000s, Russians continue to arrive in the United States seeking better lives.

In the twenty-first century, Russian Americans are an important part of American society. Bringing with them a wealth of different talents, customs, and skills, they have greatly enriched their new home.

# 1 MOTHER RUSSIA

*Russia is an enormous country. In fact, it is the largest nation in the world, sprawling across more than six million square miles of eastern Europe and northern Asia. Its capital, Moscow, lies in western Russia. Not far from Moscow is the Volga, Russia's main river and the longest waterway in Europe. Farther to the east lie the Ural Mountains, a low range that divides European Russia from the vast Asian portion of the country. Across the Urals, the steppes begin. These wide plains, covered in rich black soil, form the heart of Russia.*

## OLD COUNTRY

Russia also has a sprawling history, stretching back over many centuries. Slavic settlers—members of a large group of people who speak closely related languages—first came to the region thousands of years ago. They lived in small villages, each made up of several family groups who shared land, dwellings, and tools. Farmers grew crops including wheat, barley, rye, beets, apples, pears, and plums. They also kept livestock such as chickens, geese, and goats. As the Slavic population expanded, it gradually came to occupy large areas of eastern Europe and central Russia.

Over time, the Slavic people separated into two main groups: the western Slavs and the eastern Slavs. In response to outside rule and other factors, these two groups gradually developed differences in languages, writing systems, religion, and politics. For example, the eastern Slavs adopted a Cyrillic script (alphabet), while western Slavs wrote with the Latin letters used in western Europe and the modern United States. Most modern Russians are Slavs from the eastern group. Slavs also live in many European nations beyond Russia, including modern Poland, Serbia and Montenegro, the Czech Republic, and Bulgaria. In addition, Russia is home to many non–Slavic ethnic groups.

*Modern Russia is about twice the size of the United States, but it has a population that is half the size. Go to www.inamericabooks.com to download this map and other materials.*

## An Empire Is Born

The history of the Russian Empire begins with the growth of the city of Kiev in the ninth century A.D. Part of Ukraine in modern times, Kiev was then an important trading center because of its strategic location on the Dnieper River. In the late 800s, Oleg, a prince from Novgorod (in modern-day Russia), established Kievan Rus, the first Slavic state. Kievan Rus laid the foundation for a series of realms in what would later become Russia.

However, internal unrest and outside invaders eventually destroyed Kievan Rus. The Mongols (a group of Asian fighters and skilled horsemen) conquered Russian lands in the 1200s. The Mongols' rule eventually weakened, and in the 1400s, they were replaced by czars, powerful Russian emperors who ruled from Moscow.

To investigate Russian history, check out links at www.inamericabooks.com.

Meanwhile, Russia worked to expand its territory. In the mid-1500s, Ivan IV—usually called Ivan the Terrible for his harsh and violent rule—extended Moscow's power far to the east by conquering Kazan and Astrakhan, two Mongol territories on the Volga River. During Ivan's reign, Russia also claimed Siberia, a vast wilderness area to the northeast of Russian territory. Scattered forts in Siberia gradually grew into towns, and eastward expansion advanced steadily. Finally, in 1639, Russian fur hunters called *promyshlenniki*—who traded sable and other rich, valuable furs—crossed the Stanovoi Mountains in eastern Siberia and reached the Pacific Ocean.

Russian explorers had covered approximately 5,800 miles in sixty years, traveling through some of the world's most rugged land.

Meanwhile, Russia moved westward into Poland and the Baltic states of Lithuania, Latvia, and Estonia, and southward into Azerbaijan, where the culture of the people is closer to that of Iran and Turkey than to that of Slavic Russia. Russian expansion also engulfed the Georgians and Armenians in the area between the Black and Caspian seas. In the early 1700s, the czar Peter the Great made the neighboring Ukraine part of Russia. And during the 1700s and into the 1800s, the exploration and settlement of the land beyond the Caucasus brought many different ethnic groups under Russian control.

## RUSSIAN LIFE

Even as the Russian Empire grew and prospered, life was hard for the average Russian. From the 1500s into the mid–1800s, the great majority of Russians were farmworkers called serfs.

*During Ivan the Terrible's rule, some farmworkers called serfs fled from harsh landlords and formed their own communities and army. The army, known as the Cossacks, became famous worldwide for its fierce soldiers and skilled horsemen (above).*

# The Alaskan Venture

Most Americans think that their nation was first colonized by western Europeans who crossed the Atlantic Ocean and settled in the area along the eastern coast of North America. However, Alaska—the nation's forty-ninth state—was actually explored and settled by Russians.

Peter the Great, who became czar of Russia in 1689, was deeply interested in science and especially in European theories that North America and Asia might be joined in the north. In 1724 Peter ordered an expedition to the eastern Siberian coast to settle this question. He chose Vitus Bering, an officer in the Russian navy, to lead it.

In 1727 Bering arrived at Russia's Pacific port of Okhotsk. A short expedition by sea along the eastern coast of Siberia convinced him that Asia and North America were not linked by land. But after returning to Peter's capital at Saint Petersburg, Bering was sent back to the Pacific to find out how far away North American shores were from Siberia. In 1741 Bering finally reached North America, landing in the Aleutian Islands.

Foxes, sea otter, and seals were plentiful in and around the Aleutian Islands, and their rich furs brought high prices. Promyshlenniki (fur hunters) eager to make their fortunes soon followed Bering to the islands, setting out across the northern Pacific waters in primitive flat-bottomed boats held together by willow bark or leather straps. By 1763 Russian traders had reached Kodiak Island—almost nine thousand miles from Saint Petersburg. In 1784 Russian settlers formed a colony on Kodiak Island, and in 1799 the government founded the Russian American Company to oversee Russian trade in the region. That same year, a permanent settlement was established in New Archangel (later renamed Sitka), Alaska, and eventually the company had its own fleet of ships and traded with California, Hawaii, and the Philippines. Russia's American colonies continued to do a lively business until 1867, when Russia sold its Alaskan territories to the United States.

*Residents of Sitka, Alaska, saved many Russian Orthodox religious objects from Saint Michael the Archangel Cathedral when it burned down in 1966, and placed them in their new cathedral* (above). *The original Russian Orthodox cathedral* (inset) *was built in the 1840s—while Russia still controlled Alaska.*

Serfs did not own the land they worked. The country's farmland belonged to a relatively small number of wealthy landowners, and serfs lived and farmed on this property. Landlords provided serfs with housing and food, but both were often of poor quality, and most serfs lived in poverty. In return, the serfs provided their labor and most of the crops that they raised. Technically considered the property of the landowners, serfs were bound to the land that they worked and had very little freedom to move about within Russia or to change their economic situation.

In 1861 Czar Alexander II declared an end to the serfdom system. But even then, the average Russian citizen saw little improvement in his or her life. Most former serfs remained terribly poor. Living in small villages called mirs, they farmed land that was now owned in common by the entire village and controlled by a local council. But each plot of land was barely large enough to support a family. Peasants still struggled to make ends meet, spending long days laboring in the fields. As the population grew, land became even scarcer and the people grew still poorer.

Farming families usually lived in small homes with wooden walls and thatched roofs. These dwellings generally consisted of one room. During the bitterly cold Russian winter, calves, pigs, and other livestock sometimes shared living space with the family. A large oven usually took up a large

IT'S TIME . . . .
TO MOURN
FOR RUSSIA'S
GLOOMY
SAVOUR,
LAND WHERE
I LEARNED
TO LOVE
AND WEEP,
LAND WHERE
MY HEART IS
BURIED DEEP.

—*Alexander Pushkin, in* Eugene Onegin, *1833*

part of the home and was used for light, heat, and cooking.

A peasant family's diet was relatively limited. Most people could not afford to buy meat, so most meals were made up of dark rye bread, potatoes, dairy products, and a few fresh fruits and vegetables that could be grown during the short summer season. But these meals were a luxury compared to times when food ran short. In the late 1800s, famines (severe food shortages) killed a total of more than 400,000 rural Russians.

During this time period, a growing number of factories began rising in Moscow, Saint Petersburg, and other Russian cities. The factories offered an alternative to farming, and hundreds of peasants left their farms for the cities. But the life of a factory worker in Russia was hardly better than life in the countryside. Many employees labored twelve hours a day or more, often working seven days a week, for very low wages.

*The house I lived in was made from logs we cut in the forest, and were filled in with mud and clay. The floor was made of mud, and each Saturday we would put new clay over it to make it look clean. Sometimes we had windows, sometimes we didn't. When we did have a window it was made of paper.*

—"Mr. W" (anonymous Russian immigrant who arrived in the United States in the early 1900s), describing a Russian peasant's home in the early 1900s

Machinery in plants such as textile mills was often unsafe, and injuries were common.

Beyond the factory, living conditions were usually cramped and uncomfortable. Unmarried workers often lived in factory-provided housing. In these lodgings, workers usually slept in large, barracks-style rooms filled with many bunks, offering little privacy and few comforts. A worker could also rent a single room—or part of a room—and sometimes two or more families squeezed into a tiny apartment.

Russian peasants and workers longed to improve their lives, but they had few opportunities. One of the biggest challenges was the strict hold of the government over their lives. The czar—who was often referred to as the "father" of the Russian people—was considered the absolute lord of the land and its citizens, and the central government was all-powerful. For example, people were not allowed to leave their villages or cities without

*Nicholas II became the ruler of Russia in 1894. The czar and his family* (**above**) *led lives of luxury, while poor peasants and workers struggled to get by.*

permission, and they were not allowed to join unions (organizations for workers' rights) or political parties. Those who spoke out or acted against the czar or his policies were severely punished by his secret police, who were free to imprison anyone even vaguely suspected of disloyalty or other crimes. Even a minor violation of the law could be punished by a long exile in Siberia.

Required military service was another burden for Russian citizens. Every Russian man had to serve at least five years in the czar's army, whether the empire was at war or peace. His pay for this service was next to nothing. If he had family, they were left to manage for themselves during his absence. For Russians already struggling to pay the czar's high taxes and still feed and house their families, the loss of a household head could be devastating.

In addition, most peasants had very little education, in part because many children had to miss school or drop out completely to help their parents with farmwork or household chores. In the early 1900s, at least 50 percent of the Russian population could not sign their own names and nearly 70 percent could not read. This illiteracy limited the people's ability to challenge the government's unfair policies. With all of these limitations, finding a job somewhere other than the fields or the factory floor was nearly impossible. Facing what seemed like a hopeless future, many Russians began looking for another way. That way, for some, was moving to the United States.

## FLEEING FOR FAITH

While many Russians left their homeland to escape poverty, some groups left to find religious freedom. Among these groups were the Russian Mennonites.

The Russian Mennonites were descendants of a Dutch religious sect founded in 1530. Working as farmers, they ran their own schools and lived in their own tightly knit communities. One of the religion's main teachings was pacifism, a firm opposition to war and other violence.

LEARN MORE ABOUT MENNONITES AND CATHERINE THE GREAT BY CHECKING LINKS AT WWW.INAMERICABOOKS.COM.

The Dutch Mennonites were persecuted for their beliefs and were forced to move from place to place in Europe. In the late 1700s, they were invited to Russia by the czarina Catherine the Great, who hoped they would farm the rich land of the south and east. Although Russian Orthodoxy was the main religion in the empire, Catherine promised the Mennonites that they would be able to practice their religion freely. In addition, she did not require them to serve in the military, which would have violated their pacifist beliefs. Many Mennonites took Catherine's offer. But by the late 1800s, the Russian government's policies had changed. Russia's leaders wanted to "Russify" all of the empire's peoples. Russification aimed to reduce the differences among the Russian Empire's many cultures, ethnicities, and religions and make them all more "Russian." As part of this goal, all citizens were required to attend Russian schools, use the Russian language, and complete military service—no matter what their religion was.

In the face of these new conditions, Russian Mennonites decided to seek a new home. Many chose to move to the United States, a country known for its tradition of religious freedom. Whole Mennonite villages left Russia, and a total of approximately ten thousand Russian Mennonites moved to the United States in the last decades of the nineteenth century.

Another group that left for religious reasons was the Molokans.

The Molokans were members of a Christian sect that had broken away from the Russian Orthodox Church in the 1600s. Molokans rejected the elaborate ceremonies and symbols of Russian Orthodoxy. They worshipped in very simple churches, and their services were centered on the Bible. In addition, the Molokans, like the Mennonites, were pacifists.

The Russian government, which saw itself as the protector of Russian Orthodoxy and did not regard any

# CHURCH OF THE CROWN

The Russian Orthodox Church can trace its beginnings to the birth of Christianity. Before A.D. 1054, the eastern and western (or Orthodox and Catholic) churches coexisted peacefully and considered themselves two branches of the same church. But in 1054, a split, or schism, occurred over geographical, cultural, and political differences.

The Eastern Orthodox churches became independent of the Roman Catholic Church. The Russian Orthodox Church is a national church, and it is just one of many national branches of the Eastern Orthodox Church. When Christian Russians came to America, they brought their faith with them. Although the church represented, in some ways, the czarist system they had fled, its beliefs were powerful and deeply held.

other religion as valid, began a system of persecution against the Molokans. Molokan families were forced from central Russia and exiled to remote parts of the empire. Even there, they often faced harassment from government officials and from their Orthodox neighbors. Then, when war broke out between Russia and Japan in 1904, the Molokans faced the possibility of being forced to fight. To escape this fate, approximately five thousand Molokans decided to leave Russia for the United States.

## BEYOND THE PALE

In the late 1800s and early 1900s, large numbers of Russian Jews also began seeking an escape from Russia. For centuries, anti–Semitism (strong prejudice and discrimination against Jews) had been a problem throughout Europe. Jewish people in Russia had been harshly persecuted for many years.

Decades earlier, the Russian government had passed a law restricting Jews to an area in western Russia called the Pale of Settlement. The Pale's boundaries varied depending on the czar in power, but by 1885 the Pale was home to about four million Jews. Even within that area, their freedom was restricted. They could live only in certain towns and could not move about freely. The kinds of jobs they could hold were limited. They were not allowed to own land, but they could be merchants, peddlers, craftspeople, or tax collectors.

Despite these restrictions, Jews in Russia had held firmly to their traditional way of life. They celebrated their own holy days with ancient customs, and their

I REMEMBER A TIME WHEN I THOUGHT A POGROM [FIERCE ANTI-JEWISH RIOT] HAD BROKEN OUT IN OUR STREET, AND I WONDER THAT I DID NOT DIE OF FEAR. . . . GATES WERE LOCKED; SHUTTERS WERE BARRED. . . . FEARFUL AND YET CURIOUS, WE LOOKED THROUGH THE CRACKS IN THE SHUTTERS.

—*Mary Antin, who left Russia in 1894, in* The Promised Land children went to Hebrew schools. Literacy was common among Jews at a time when most Russian peasants could neither read nor write.

But in the late 1800s and early 1900s, as religious and ethnic minorities in Russia faced a period of growing repression, discrimination, and violence, Jews were persecuted especially harshly. Pogroms (fierce anti–Jewish riots) erupted frequently. Russian citizens formed armed mobs that attacked Jewish communities—often as the army and police looked on. Pogroms left homes, businesses, and synagogues (Jewish places of worship) looted and destroyed, and hundreds of people dead, wounded, and homeless. Fearing for their lives, more than one million Russian Jews decided to make the journey to the New World between 1880 and 1910. They left Russia with the dream that America would offer them the chance to live and work in peace.

*This visitor to New York City's Ellis Island Immigration Museum stands by a 1905 photograph showing the funeral of a man killed during a pogrom in Kishinev. (Kishinev, once part of the Russian Empire, is located in present-day Moldova, a nation west of Ukraine.) The visitor's father is shown in the photograph (**front row, far right**). For links to the museum and to information about pogroms, visit www.inamericabooks.com.*

## THE FIRST WAVE

For all of these reasons—poverty, injustice, religious persecution, and ethnic discrimination—many people strove to escape from czarist Russia in the late nineteenth and early twentieth centuries.

But emigration (leaving one's country) was a long and often challenging process. For example, filling out the required passport application was a difficult task for many peasants, who were often unable to read and write. And the application fee, combined with the cost of the trip itself, totaled more than one hundred dollars—a huge amount for the average Russian. For those who couldn't get official permission, leaving the country illegally was an option. But that path required bribing officials, an expensive option that the average peasant or worker could not afford.

Nevertheless, close to two million people—most of them Russian Jews—did make the journey from the Russian Empire to the

*For many of the first Russian emigrants, the trip to the United States began on a long train trip to the border of their country. Many traveled in crowded, unfurnished boxcars.*

United States between about 1880 and 1914. To raise money for the trip, many peasants sold nearly all of their possessions—which were usually few enough to begin with. Packing small bags and suitcases, they said farewell to their homes and to any relatives staying behind. Then they boarded trains bound for port cities hundreds of miles away. Most Russians sailed from Hamburg, Germany, one of Europe's busiest hubs of emigration to North America. Many others left from coastal cities in France.

Already weary from the days-long trip, Russians finally reached their ports. There they were crowded into the steerage—a lower-deck area—on ships bound for America. Steerage tickets were the cheapest fares on passenger ships. But the steerage was a dark, cramped, and miserable place to spend the journey across the Atlantic Ocean, which lasted up to two weeks or longer, depending on the conditions. The air grew stale and heavy. When the seas were rough, many people became sick. The food was usually terrible, and the sleeping arrangements were uncomfortable and without privacy.

Through it all, Russian immigrants must have held tightly to their dream of new lives in America. They did not know exactly what lay ahead, but they knew what they were leaving behind—poverty, persecution, and hopelessness. In the New World, they would have the chance to begin again.

# 2 BETWEEN TWO WORLDS

*In the late 1800s, New York City's harbor was filled with ships arriving from Europe. From the decks of these great oceangoing vessels, immigrants could see the Statue of Liberty—a symbol of the new life they hoped to find in the United States.*

But most Russian immigrants were not able to enter the New World just yet. Beginning in 1892, nearly all immigrants traveling in steerage had to go through the Ellis Island Immigration Station, located on a small island in New York's harbor. At that time, immigration to the United States—not just from Russia but from Italy, China, and many other countries—was skyrocketing. The Ellis Island station was built to handle this large number of new immigrants as they arrived.

The first step for Russians at the immigration station was a medical exam. A doctor checked each person for signs of physical or mental disease. If someone did have an illness, he or she could be kept at the station until they recovered. If the medical condition was very serious, an immigrant could even be returned to Russia.

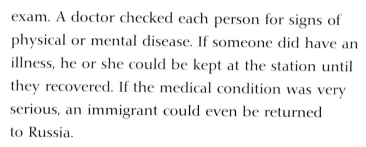

*Russian and Polish passengers on this ship roll up their sleeves to receive vaccination shots. Sometimes, Ellis Island was so busy that its doctors boarded ships to examine passengers.*

Russian immigrants also had to speak to station officials. Often they had to wait for many hours before seeing someone. When it was their turn, they were asked many questions about how much money they had, whether they had relatives in the United States, if they had jobs waiting for them, and other practical matters. Because most Russians did not

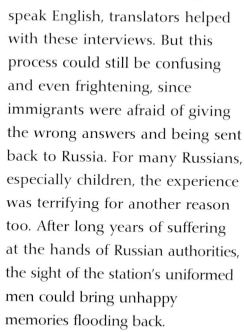

speak English, translators helped with these interviews. But this process could still be confusing and even frightening, since immigrants were afraid of giving the wrong answers and being sent back to Russia. For many Russians, especially children, the experience was terrifying for another reason too. After long years of suffering at the hands of Russian authorities, the sight of the station's uniformed men could bring unhappy memories flooding back.

When Russian immigrants were approved to enter the United States, they left Ellis Island and finally got their first real taste of their new home. Newly arrived immigrants were weary after their long journey. Overwhelmed by the noise, activity, and new sights of bustling New York City, they felt lost and afraid. While some arrived with their families, many others came alone. These were usually single men who hoped either to return to Russia one day or to bring their wives and children, if they had any, to the United States eventually.

Some arrivals stayed in New York or nearby states such as Pennsylvania and New Jersey. But for others, the trip was not yet over. Smaller numbers of Russians traveled beyond the East Coast region to settle in the Southeast, the Midwest, or the West Coast.

But no matter where they ended up, new Russian immigrants were eager to begin building their new lives in America. And whatever their reasons had been for leaving Russia for the United States, they shared many of the same challenges once they arrived, as well as the same basic desires: jobs, homes, and a better future.

## "HE WHO DOESN'T WORK, DOESN'T EAT"

One of the first and most pressing needs for Russian immigrants was finding work. Most arrived nearly penniless. The average peasant had few job skills other than farming and little or no knowledge of the English language—making it very difficult to find a good job. Desperate to feed themselves and their families, many Russians were willing to take low-paying, difficult, and even dangerous jobs.

WHEN I CAME HERE I COULD SPEAK NO ENGLISH AT ALL, AND THE ONLY THING I KNEW HOW TO DO WAS WORK. . . . I GOT A JOB IN THE PACKING HOUSE KILLING COWS. I WORKED 16 TO 17 HOURS A DAY AND MADE MAYBE TWENTY CENTS AN HOUR WHEN I STARTED.

—"Mr. L" (anonymous Russian immigrant who arrived in the United States in the early 1900s)

Large numbers of Russians settled in New York and Pennsylvania, where many found work in steel mills and coal mines. Other industries that employed Russians included meatpacking, sugar refining, and cotton, wool, and other textile mills. Some Russian Jews became peddlers, as they had been in Russia, selling any goods that they could, or they continued to practice a craft such as needlework. Women were often so busy caring for children, preparing food, and doing other household chores that they hardly had time to work outside the home. Nevertheless, many did take jobs to help earn extra income. In mining towns, some women kept chickens and sold the eggs, while others took in sewing and mending work. Many Russian women in bigger cities found jobs in the growing garment industry. Ten or more garment workers often crowded into one factory room, making coats, pants, and other clothing for as many as seventeen hours a day. These factories, often called sweatshops, were terribly hot in the summer, and they were a health and fire hazard at all times.

Because of their limited language skills and job experience, Russians usually were assigned the most difficult—and dangerous—tasks at their jobs, especially in the mining and manufacturing industries. Deep

*Peer into the subterranean kingdom of the mines, into those places where God's light does not penetrate and . . . what figures will you see there, often knee-deep in cold water, bent over or prone, in narrow passages, covered with mud, choking from dust and harmful gases, threatened every minute by a thousand dangers?*

—from a 1914 letter in Russkaya Zemlya (Russian Soil), a Russian-language newspaper in New York City, writing of Russian immigrant miners in the coal mines, light was dim and the air was thick with the coal dust that left many miners coughing. Some eventually suffered from lung disease. The steel mills were no better. Their furnaces were fed by the same coal that other Russians mined, and men working in chambers almost too hot to bear lifted heavy sacks of the fuel and hurled them into blazing ovens.

And the hours were long. Laborers in steel mills usually worked twelve-hour shifts seven days a week. Every two weeks, when work shifts were changed, they often had to work for eighteen or even twenty-four hours at a time. When one Russian man was asked to describe his week, he said that he had worked ninety-one hours, and spent what little was left of his time

*Carnegie Steel Company's factory in Homestead, Pennsylvania, employed many Russian immigrants. As seen in this 1890s photo, the factory filled the air with thick, dirty smoke.*

simply eating, sleeping, and traveling to and from work. On top of the brutal work and the grueling hours, pay was dismally low. In 1909 Russian workers earned an average of just $2.06 a day. Some earned as little as $5.00 per week. American-born workers in the same jobs often earned twice that amount.

Because they often did dangerous work—frequently while exhausted—many Russian laborers were involved in accidents. But even when they were injured, they did not always get the help and the money that they needed—and that their jobs were supposed to provide. There were few laws to protect workers at that time, and Russian workers were often unfamiliar with those that did exist. Employers rarely took the time or the trouble to help them learn, often caring little for the welfare of their workers. In addition to other hardships, Russian immigrants often had to put up with strict, prejudiced, and even cruel bosses. These men were feared for their power to hire and fire employees. But they were also hated by the workers who endured their harassment and insults.

Facing such terrible conditions, some Russians took an interest in U.S. labor unions. But poverty and language again proved to be obstacles. The most successful unions at the time were those whose members were skilled craftspeople such as bricklayers or carpenters. But most Russians were unskilled laborers who still struggled to have their unions recognized. Others could not afford to pay union fees on their small salaries. However, a number of Russians did join the United Mine Workers of America, the Union of Russian Workers, and the Industrial Workers of the World (IWW). Russian union members took part in the Homestead Steel Strike in Pennsylvania in 1892, in the anthracite coal strike in 1902, and in a Chicago slaughterhouse strike in 1904. David Dubinsky, a Russian Jewish immigrant, helped form the International Ladies' Garment Workers' Union (ILGWU). Under his leadership, the ILGWU built low–cost apartments and established health centers, nurseries, summer camps, and adult education classes.

*David Dubinsky led the International Ladies' Garment Workers' Union for thirty-four years before he retired in 1966.*

Due largely to the efforts of leaders such as Dubinsky, working and living conditions gradually did improve for Russians and for all American workers.

## A ROOF AND A STOVE

For Russian immigrants, who could barely scrape by on their low wages, finding housing was a big concern. By the early 1900s, many newcomers had family or friends already in the United States with whom they could often stay, at least temporarily. Even when they moved out, they usually stayed in the same area. In New York City, Philadelphia, Chicago, and other cities, Russian immigrants tended to settle near one another. By the end of the twentieth century, the main centers of Russian American populations had Russian neighborhoods. One of the largest was New York City's Lower East Side, where many Jewish immigrants settled.

*Russian immigrants shop a Lower East Side market in New York in the early 1900s. Visit www.inamericabooks.com to find links about immigrant life on the Lower East Side.*

Living near other Russians helped make immigrants feel more at home. But these neighborhoods were often the worst in town. Rent was cheap, but conditions were miserable. In New York and other big cities, shabby, rundown apartments called tenements housed most immigrants. In these dark, dank buildings, a two- or three-room apartment was often home to five people or more. Residents usually had to share a bathroom with several other families, and some had no access at all to bathtubs. The little light that came through one or two small, cloudy windows was made even dimmer by the smoky coal stoves that many people used for heat and cooking, and by washing hung to dry in the middle of the room. Cracked walls often let freezing drafts in during the winter, while poor ventilation made most apartments miserably hot in the summer.

In smaller towns, coal miners generally rented small homes near the mines that they worked. These dwellings were usually little more than small one-room shacks built of reused wood and scrap metal. Toilets were usually outside in shared, run-down outhouses, and some homes had no running water. Single miners also lived in barracks similar to those that factory workers in Russia had known.

Living in such conditions, Russians—most of whom had been farmers in their homeland—found themselves missing the vast open spaces and clear air of their Russian villages. Some did move westward in the United States, finding work in farming communities or other rural settings. There was more space in the countryside, and people were often able to build homes that were sturdier, cleaner, and brighter than anything they could afford in the city. But they were also farther from other Russians and lacked the community and support of their fellow immigrants.

In addition to the challenge of finding jobs and homes, Russian immigrants had to deal with unscrupulous people who took advantage of their inexperience in the United States. For example, private banks sometimes made deals with corrupt lawyers to cheat immigrants out of part of their savings. Other, more everyday problems included grocers who charged newcomers higher prices for foods—which were usually not as fresh or as high-quality as those sold in stores where Americans shopped. A poor diet only worsened health problems caused by living conditions, overwork, and hour after hour of breathing smoky, dusty factory air. Russians were often ill. But few could afford good medical care. And after years of distrusting the Russian government, they were often suspicious of government-run public clinics in the United States. Instead, many people went to questionable doctors, or "quacks." Even these doctors charged immigrants high fees for treatment and sold them expensive—but often worthless—medicines.

## DO NOT LET YOUR BABY CRY

EVERY RUSSIAN MOTHER knows that the only certain medicine for the crying and discomfort and sleeplessness of her baby is "Romko," manufactured by the Baby Safety Company. Do not let your baby cry and suffer for hours. . . . do not wait one minute, but buy in the local drug store, for thirty-five cents, a bottle of "Romko."

—*from an ad for a medicine marketed to Russian Americans in the early 1900s*

# FARM LIFE IN THE NEW WORLD

One of the largest groups to settle in the U.S. countryside and work as farmers were the Russian Mennonites. Starting a farm was difficult. Unable to speak English and unfamiliar with U.S. laws and customs, Russian immigrants could not always find good farming plots. Many made arrangements before leaving Russia, but they were often cheated by dishonest agents who sold them poor land. In addition, most Mennonites had to borrow money from banks and business organizations to establish their farms.

Soon after arriving in the United States, most Mennonite families boarded trains to Kansas, Nebraska, the Dakotas, and Minnesota.

*New arrivals to central Kansas in the early twentieth century, Russian Mennonite families temporarily live together in a barn.*

In the town nearest the land they planned to farm, they bought a wagon, horses, and farm tools. Then they set out with their families to their new home—often in the midst of tall, dry grass and barren prairie with no road in sight. The idea of making something out of the emptiness must have been a little frightening, but the newcomers were experienced farmers. When they had good soil, they could make a farm prosper. Carrying seeds over from Russia, they planted "winter wheat," which grew even during cool weather. They also worked to repay their loans as soon as they could. The Mennonites were soon known for being trustworthy and hard working, and their neighbors generally thought highly of them.

Back in Russia, farming villages had been made up of houses built on a single main street, with nearby farmland divided into small, neighboring strips. In the United States, however, farms were miles apart, and immigrants missed having friends close by. Nevertheless, Russian Mennonites remained a tightly knit community based on their common heritage and strong faith. They founded churches and schools in their new home and kept their customs alive.

Many Molokan immigrants also tried their hand at farming in the United States. Most had first settled in California, with the largest population in the heart of Los Angeles. There they tried to create a community that felt like their old Russian villages. However, they discovered that it was difficult to preserve their unique culture amid the hustle and bustle of modern city life. Feeling that their traditions were being destroyed, some Molokans left Los Angeles and established small rural communities in California, as well as in Oregon and other western states. Others stayed in the city and founded their own churches and other community organizations.

## FEELING AT HOME

Although life in America was far from easy, Russian immigrants also found its bright spots. When they felt isolated or lonely, they could turn to their neighbors for company and cheer. While they sometimes had trouble relating to Americans, who could seem cold and unfeeling, fellow Russians offered understanding and warmth. In a country where the language was unfamiliar, they could speak Russian or Yiddish (a Jewish language related to German) with their friends and relatives.

During the little free time they had, Russians enjoyed gathering to talk about memories of the old country and to share favorite traditional foods such as borscht (beet soup) and *pelmeni* (meat-filled dumplings). Visiting with one another was a way to unwind and find a break from the routine of hard work. Other pastimes included playing cards, listening to Russian music, going to movies, and attending dances and other social events.

*From places far away,
the river Volga flows.
The river Volga flows,
it flows on endlessly.
Through fields of
golden grain,
And 'cross the plain.
The river Volga flows,
and I am seventeen.
And mother said, life can
bring many things.
You may grow weary of
your wanderings.
And when you come back
home at journey's end,
Into the Volga's waters,
dip your hands.*

—*from a folk song
popular with Russian
immigrants in the
early 1900s*

Many Russians also found comfort in their religion. Russian Jews were glad to find the freedom to practice their religion, to work

*This painting of Mary and the infant Jesus, "Our Lady of Sitka," has been part of Saint Michael the Archangel Cathedral in Sitka, Alaska since 1850.*

in the jobs they chose, and to educate their children in their religious tradition. Some spent their Friday evenings at local synagogues, followed by a traditional meal shared with relatives and neighbors. Orthodox Christians turned to their faith too. For centuries the Russian Orthodox Church had been one of the few constants in Russia. Russian Orthodox services, with their familiar rituals, icons (religious paintings), and music, helped immigrants find stability in their new homes as well.

In addition to providing spiritual comfort, Russian American religious organizations also offered practical aid. For example, Jewish loan associations helped Russian Jewish immigrants who were extremely poor or sick. These private groups lent small sums of money to those in need. This

*In the mid-1700s, Catherine the Great invited some German families to farm in southern Russia. Several generations later, some of these immigrants, including this family posing for a photograph in late nineteenth-century Colorado, moved to the United States.*

tradition of receiving help from acquaintances rather than depending on charity was rooted in Jewish communities in Russia. Most of those who borrowed money from the loan associations paid them back as soon as they could, which made that money available for someone else in need. Similarly, the Russian

OUR CHILDREN HAVE BEEN RUINED BY AMERICAN CUSTOMS. WE CAME FROM THE OLD COUNTRY AND WORKED LIKE DOGS TO EDUCATE AND PROVIDE FOR OUR KIDS. THEN THEY GOT MARRIED AND MOVED AWAY. THEY WERE ASHAMED OF US BECAUSE WE DIDN'T SPEAK ENGLISH WELL AND DIDN'T HAVE NICE THINGS.

—"Mr. F" (a Russian immigrant to the United States in the early 1900s)

Orthodox Catholic Mutual Aid Society ran orphanages, helped pay for medical bills, and offered other assistance to members.

Family was another source of strength for Russian immigrants. Mothers, daughters, and granddaughters were usually especially close, just as they had been in Russia. However, young Russian Americans did not always see eye to eye with their parents. Many children of immigrants went to U.S. schools and learned English quickly, although some had to drop out and help support the family by working. As time went by, they became more and more "Americanized," while their parents often clung to Russian traditions. Russian American youths sometimes disagreed with their parents' religious customs and preferred American ways, such as independent dating—ideas that sometimes shocked the older generation. In Russia girls were closely chaperoned. Sometimes, in the case of traditional marriages arranged by parents, a Russian woman did not even meet her husband until their wedding day. In America, young Russians often found that they liked the idea of choosing their spouses themselves. And young married couples often moved away from their families in America, while in Russia they had almost always remained in the same town—or even in the same household.

But even as Russian American children and teenagers found new interests and explored new ideas, they also respected important values from their homeland. For example, most young Russian Jews still had a deep respect for learning. Working in factories and small shops to earn money for college, many succeeded in becoming teachers, physicians, lawyers, and other professionals. Other Russians also worked hard to escape poverty, and many helped their parents with money and other gifts.

## REVOLUTION

As the first wave of Russian immigrants settled into American life, World War I (1914–1918) broke out in Europe. Three years later, the United States entered the conflict, and soon saw that a volunteer army would not provide enough soldiers for such a large war. In response, the U.S. Congress issued a draft requiring young, able-bodied men to join the armed forces. For Russian Mennonites and Molokans in the United States, this development brought back old problems. Most Americans supported the war, and when members of these pacifist communities refused to take part, newspapers and even their

American neighbors called them cowards and traitors. Many were arrested, and some were forced into military service against their will.

Other Russian immigrants also served in the war, either by joining the army voluntarily or by being drafted. At the same time, Russians in America carefully followed news of the war from their homeland. Germany had declared war on Russia on August 1, 1914, and Russia had drafted approximately 16 million men into its army. Most had inadequate equipment and little or no training. Nearly all were very poorly paid. Meanwhile, the Russian people suffered severe shortages of food, fuel, and housing. In early March 1917, centuries of unrest and discontent erupted. The Russian people revolted against the czar, and in the violent riots that followed, Czar Nicholas II was forced to give up his throne. He and his family were then executed by the revolutionaries.

The Russian Revolution was followed by a series of temporary governments as political groups competed for power. At the same time, soviets were established throughout Russia. In some places, these councils of workers, peasants, or soldiers served as the only local government during a period of confusion and lawlessness.

As time went on, Communists came to dominate many soviets. Communism is an economic and social theory based on the idea of shared property and resources and a government run by the people. The Communists' promises of "peace, bread, and land" sounded hopeful to Russians who had endured miserable poverty and injustice under czarism, and the movement gained many followers. Their beliefs would change the lives of Russians—and Russian Americans—forever.

EXPLORE COMMUNISM AND THE RUSSIAN REVOLUTION THROUGH LINKS AT WWW.INAMERICABOOKS.COM.

# 3 WAVES OF CHANGE

*In November 1917, the Bolsheviks, a party of Communist revolutionaries, seized power in Russia. They formed a new government headed by Bolshevik leader V. I. Lenin. Lenin withdrew Russia from World War I in 1918, but two years of civil war followed between the Communist Red Army and the "White" army, made up of people who opposed the new government.*

As the Communists tried to establish a "workers' government" thousands of miles away, Russian Americans followed the momentous developments in their motherland with great interest.

Many wondered if Russia had finally found a system of government that would meet the needs and desires of all of its people. Perhaps the new government really would do

*From a speaker's stand in Moscow, Vladimir Ilich Lenin (upper left) addresses a Russian crowd shortly after the 1917 Russian Revolution.*

something to correct the ills of the czarist regime, they thought. Proud of their homeland's new direction, Russians in America also felt new pride in their identity.

## DEATH OF AN ERA

At the same time, the revolution changed Russian emigration. Many poor Russians were optimistic about the new government and chose to stay in the country. On the other hand, those who had opposed the Bolsheviks risked losing their fortunes and often their lives if they remained in Communist Russia.

Immediately after the revolution, many wealthy people fled. As time went on, the Communists set up a new secret police force that arrested, imprisoned, or killed anyone whom the government considered counterrevolutionary, or opposed to the Communist revolution. More and more Russians who disagreed with the Communists braved great danger to leave. More than twenty thousand came to the United States, forming the second large wave of Russian immigration to the United States. While many earlier emigrants had left their country in search of food and religious freedom, more of the new emigrants came to the United States seeking political freedom.

World War I had left Russia's transportation routes in ruin, and the people who managed to flee to the United States did so in roundabout ways. Some left from southern Russia and came to the United States via Turkey. Others went westward from Leningrad (the name the Communists had given Saint Petersburg) or Moscow all the way to Vladivostok on the Pacific coast. They crossed the ocean much as the first Russians in Alaska had done.

Once in the United States, the new immigrants faced common problems. Some had been able to hold onto at least a portion of their riches. They were able to live in relative comfort in their new country. But many others were penniless, just as the immigrants of the 1800s had been, and desperately in need of jobs. However, many of these Russians had never worked. Their families had been wealthy, and

IT WAS A NEW WORLD. MOST OF THE FORMER RUSSIAN NOBILITY, SUDDENLY OUT IN THE COLD, . . . HADN'T THE FIRST IDEA OF HOW TO MAKE A LIVING. OUTSIDE OF CARD-PLAYING, HORSE-RIDING, AND A FLUENCY IN FRENCH, THEY HAD NO SKILLS TO SPEAK OF.

—*Alex Shoumatoff in* Russian Blood, *describing immigrants who fled the Russian Revolution of 1917* they had lived on large country estates or in luxurious city mansions with many servants. Others had held highly respected jobs in Russia but suddenly found themselves without work. People who had once been nobles, officers, university professors, and government officials had to earn a living in the United States.

Most of the immigrants in this wave settled in the Russian American communities that had been formed earlier. Many were able to find jobs as waiters and maids in restaurants and hotels. Some became butlers, cooks, and chauffeurs in wealthy homes. Those who had worked at universities often learned English and found teaching jobs in the United States. A princess who had enjoyed doing needlework in Russia sold quilts, and a former officer in the czar's army opened a riding academy.

*Some Russian immigrants arriving at Ellis Island in the early twentieth century had been wealthy before the Russian Revolution of 1917.*

## SEEING RED

Many of the Russians who fled the revolution of 1917 looked with longing and sadness at the changing Russia. It seemed to some immigrants as though their homeland might be closed to them forever. Yet even as they worked to build new lives in their new country, they held deep pride in their ancestry and traditions.

However, the revolution and the rise of Communism also led to unexpected difficulties between Russians and other Americans. The U.S. government and most Americans were anti–Communist. They saw the new system and its philosophy as directly opposed to American ideals of democracy and capitalism (an economic system based on free trade and private ownership). U.S. leaders cut off friendly relations with Russia's government and criticized the nation's direction.

At the same time, many U.S. officials were seized by a "Red Scare"—an extreme fear of Communism and of anyone suspected of holding Communist views. The government grew increasingly suspicious of Russian immigrants, afraid that they might be Communist spies or involved in Communist plots.

Some Russian immigrants were, in fact, Communists or members of other organizations that Americans

> *Since the "Bolshevik" régime began in Russia, the Russian is regarded everywhere as a "Bolshevik" and is shunned. . . . When he seeks new employment he is inevitably met with the suspicion that he is a "Bolshevik" and he goes on hunting for a job and in his soul grows and grows a spirit of revolt.*
>
> —Harvey Anderson, in charge of a YMCA program for Russians in America, ca. 1919

*Looking for proof of Communist activities in 1919, police officers searched the office of a Russian American group.*

saw as threatening. Some had brought their political convictions with them from Russia, while others had adopted them during years of hardship in the United States. Some workers belonged to the IWW, a union that was known for its radical political views. Other Russian immigrants helped publish local newspapers that sometimes discussed Communist ideas. However, many more were not associated with the Communist Party at all.

Nevertheless, the entire Russian American community was judged harshly during the Red Scare. Government leaders passed new laws against providing aid to the enemies of the United States and plotting against the U.S. military. Even speaking out against the government was also outlawed—a limitation on free speech that reminded many Russians of the government they had fled from. Using these laws, officials and police officers in the grip of the scare rounded up hundreds of Communists and other "suspects"—most of whom were targeted only because they were Russians or other European immigrants. Between November 1919 and April 1920, more than fifteen thousand people were arrested. And because the police rarely had warrants for these raids, the police violated the rights of the people they arrested. Some people were held briefly before being released, while others were jailed for extended periods and several hundred were deported (sent back to their home countries).

Many average Americans also were seized by the Red Scare. As it spread from person to person and town to town, many Russians—and especially Russian Jews—suffered prejudice and unfair treatment. Newspapers fed hatred by publishing vicious political cartoons with titles such as "Deporting the Reds." Suspicious employers fired workers simply because they were Russian, and immigrants were refused service in some shops. Russian schoolchildren were harassed by classmates who called them names. Many Russians felt bitter and resentful of Americans for treating them this way.

VISIT LINKS AT WWW.INAMERICABOOKS.COM TO DISCOVER MORE ABOUT THE RED SCARE.

However, while the Red Scare stirred up intense fear and conflict, it also faded relatively quickly. By the 1920s, Russians had worked hard to become members of their new society. Many had served their country in World War I by joining the armed forces or by working in war-related industries. Over time—and especially after the arrival of new immigrants following the Russian Revolution— Russians had expanded the kinds of jobs they held. Some had started successful restaurants or shops.

Many writers and other educated people had also joined the Russian community in the United States, and more people spoke English. Bit by bit, Russian Americans were becoming more accepted by their fellow Americans.

## STALIN'S REFUGEES

Meanwhile, the situation back in Russia continued to develop. By 1922 Lenin had succeeded in making the Communist Party the governing body of Russia and of the entire Soviet Union. The Soviet Union was a new nation made up of Russia and several neighboring republics. After Lenin's death, Joseph Stalin became the dictator of the Soviet Union in 1927.

Stalin's rule was harsh. Aiming to increase agricultural and industrial production dramatically, he drove peasants and workers to exhaustion. In addition, he strove to eliminate all opposition, going even further than the czars had to stamp out what he saw as potential threats to his power. Stalin severely limited individual freedoms and harshly persecuted ethnic and religious minorities. Soviet citizens who spoke out against Stalin's regime—or who were even suspected of speaking out—could

*For being a straight-A student, I was getting a "Stalin stipend"— a hundred rubles a month. That was great—I could go to the market and spend it all on a loaf of bread, so my sister and I could have our fill of bread that day. I still remember these thick warm slices smelling of human body—the workers at the factory would sneak them under their clothes to pass the factory checkpoint.*

*—"Genya" (anonymous Russian immigrant who came to the United States in the 1990s)*

*In Siberia in the 1930s, a Soviet guard adjusts a prisoner's chains.*

be arrested, sent to Siberian gulags (hard–labor camps), or killed. Millions died under Stalin's rule. Through it all, emigration was forbidden. The few people who did manage to leave the country were known as defectors and were, essentially, illegal escapees.

Just as Russian Americans had closely followed the exciting news of the revolution, they watched with sadness as Russia suffered under Stalin. Then, in 1939, World War II erupted between the Axis powers (Germany, Italy, Japan, and others) and the Allies (mainly Great Britain, France, the United States, and the Soviet Union). When Germany's Nazi forces invaded the Soviet Union in June 1941, some Russians fled eastward. Those who remained behind faced grim fates. Jews captured by German forces were taken to concentration camps, where most of them were killed. Thousands of other Russians were sent to Germany or German–occupied countries to do forced labor. Considered by Nazis to be ethnically inferior to Germans, Russian workers were brutally treated and poorly fed. And those who served in the Soviet army faced bitterly harsh conditions. Short on food, weapons, and other supplies, soldiers were desperate to escape. But disloyalty to Stalin and his military meant certain death—sometimes for a soldier's family as well as himself.

The Allies won the war in 1945. By the time the conflict ended, the Soviet Union had expanded its territory in Asia and Eastern Europe. But more than twenty million of its citizens were dead, and millions more had been uprooted from their homes. Many of these people were prisoners of war, forced laborers, and refugees. Most went back to the Soviet Union, but thousands were terrified of returning to the nightmare of Stalin's Russia. Nevertheless, the Soviet government demanded that all Soviet citizens be sent home. At first, Allied soldiers helping in the chaos of the war's aftermath did send Russians back to the Soviet Union, as part of an international

*More than two hundred Russian women, whom the German Nazis had enslaved during World War II, greet their U.S. Army liberators in August 1944.*

> *My father and mother and I just grabbed what clothing we could as we passed the tents where we lived, and ran to hide in the mountains. We could hear truck motors and noise from the main camp; but it died out by evening. No one was left there by then. And of course no one who fled returned there.*
>
> *—"Lara" (anonymous Russian immigrant), whose family fled an Austrian refugee camp in 1945 to avoid being sent back to the Soviet Union*

postwar agreement. By the autumn of 1945, however, a new policy was in effect. Suddenly, thousands of displaced Soviet citizens had the rare chance to emigrate.

With so many displaced persons looking for new homes, the United States opened its doors to allow the entrance of these refugees. In the years following the end of the war, approximately twenty thousand Russian immigrants from the Soviet Union arrived in the United States.

A great deal of planning went into helping these refugees settle in America, making this wave of Russian immigration very different from earlier periods. Once, a family might put a few belongings into a trunk and simply set out for the unknown. But most of these new immigrants were interviewed by American representatives before even leaving the European refugee camps. To help match people to jobs in the United States, these representatives asked potential immigrants about their experience and interests. It was fairly easy to find spots for skilled workers such as toolmakers, mechanics, and housepainters. The United States was facing a postwar labor shortage and especially welcomed workers of this type. In addition, these employees could usually do their jobs well with limited language skills. However, people such as teachers and doctors had a harder time. They needed to know more English and often had to pass tests before they could practice their professions in the United States. Similarly, lawyers had to learn not only the language but also the laws of their adopted country. Some people in these professions would have to accept work in other fields.

Once jobs had been lined up for them in the United States, workers and their families had medical examinations. Then they were given travel documents for transportation to the United States. While they waited to depart, some people took English lessons or classes about American culture. Finally, they were able to leave for their new nation and their new home.

When this group of immigrants arrived in the United States, they went wherever their jobs were. As a result, they tended to be spread out across the country rather than being concentrated in the areas where earlier Russian immigrants lived. The government often helped these new arrivals find a place to live, which lifted one burden off a newcomer's shoulders. But without the close-knit communities that had helped earlier Russians preserve their habits and traditions, many new immigrants felt lonely. In addition, many refugees had spent years in camps, had been forced to move frequently, and had experienced the mental and physical anguish of a terrible war. At first, it seemed that these new Russian immigrants had little in common with their American neighbors. But as the years passed, the refugees—like thousands of immigrants before them—grew new roots. Life and its everyday problems soon loomed larger than the shadows of the past.

## COLD SHOULDER

Although the United States and the Soviet Union had been on the same side in World War II, afterward their relationship worsened. U.S. leaders were still anti-Communist, and disapproved of Stalin's dictatorship. The Soviet government felt no more kindly about the United States and its policies. In the late 1940s, these tensions developed into a unique

*Cold War tension was very serious, but it was sometimes expressed humorously. In 1961 the U.S. space program put a chimp, Ham, in space. At Cape Canaveral, Florida (above left), Ham models his space suit. In a staged photograph taken some months after Ham's achievement, his cousin Kokomo Jr. (right) seems to think it stinks that the Russians (Soviets) launched the first man into space.*

conflict called the Cold War (1945–1991). It got this name because fighting—or "hot" war—never broke out between the two countries. However, both sides competed for power in other parts of the world, as well as racing to beat each other to goals such as landing a person on the moon. Much more frightening, however, the two countries also built large numbers of weapons including nuclear bombs. If a major nuclear war erupted, it could potentially destroy almost all life on Earth.

The hostility between their new nation and their homeland reminded many Russians of the Red Scare a few decades earlier. So did the fear that surrounded them. Terrified of nuclear war, Americans once again began to see Communism and the Soviet Union as evil and dangerous. When a senator named Joseph McCarthy set out to root out Communists working for the U.S. government, the paranoia and discrimination of the Red Scare returned. Russian Americans were not the only people targeted, but they felt especially vulnerable to suspicion and unfair accusations.

Meanwhile, emigration from the Soviet Union was limited. Even after Stalin's death in 1953, the Communist government severely restricted its citizens' movement, both inside and outside of the country.

Beginning in the 1960s, however, Russians once again began leaving their homeland in greater numbers. Many were Jews who, like those who'd left in the previous century, especially hoped to find religious freedom. Thousands left after 1975, when Jewish organizations and other international groups pressured the Soviet government to allow its Jewish population the freedom to emigrate. Most settled in Israel, but a small number made their way to the United States.

In addition to Soviet Jews who emigrated legally, other emigrants—of all religions—left without the permission of the Soviet government. Many were artists and performers who fled the country to escape restrictions on their lives and careers. In particular, a number of prominent ballet dancers, such as Rudolf Nureyev and Natalia Makarova, defected for these reasons.

WWW.

MANY PEOPLE ARE INTERESTED IN LEARNING ABOUT THEIR FAMILY'S HISTORY. THIS STUDY IS CALLED GENEALOGY. IF YOU'D LIKE TO LEARN ABOUT YOUR OWN GENEALOGY AND HOW YOUR ANCESTORS CAME TO AMERICA, VISIT WWW.INAMERICABOOKS.COM FOR TIPS AND LINKS TO HELP YOU GET STARTED.

# SENT AWAY

Some Russians did not leave their homeland voluntarily but were exiled, or forced to leave, because they criticized the Soviet system. The most famous of these political exiles, or dissidents, was the Nobel-Prize-winning author Alexander Solzhenitsyn *(right)*. His writings—especially *The Gulag Archipelago*, which described the horrific conditions of the Siberian labor camps—led to his expulsion from the Soviet Union in 1974. Solzhenitsyn eventually settled in Vermont. Other exiles who came to the United States included the poet Joseph Brodsky and the mathematician Alexander Esenin-Volpin.

Many of these people had been politically active and outspoken in the Soviet Union. They had worked toward ending restrictions on freedom of speech and other rights for Russian citizens. Even after their exile, most continued to write and speak about problems in the Soviet Union, and many also hoped to return someday to help build a freer society in their homeland. At the same time, they brought new points of view and new talents to their communities in the United States.

## LOOKING FORWARD

By the 1980s, the Soviet Union was in serious trouble. Despite the promise that many Russians had seen in Communism, the system had failed. Rather than giving all citizens equal rights and equal resources, the government had concentrated power and wealth in the hands of high-ranking members of the Communist Party. In addition, years of high spending on weapons and other expenses in the Cold War had badly weakened the Soviet economy. Poor harvests had led to food shortages, and many Russians had to stand in line for hours just to get a loaf or two of bread. The country's involvement in wars in Africa, Asia, and the Middle East had cost money and lives. And as Communism grew more and more unpopular, the Soviet government had few friends to turn to. Even the new, more open policies of

*Waiting in a long line to enter a store was a common experience for Russians throughout the twentieth century. This mid-century photograph was taken in Leningrad.*

Soviet leader Mikhail Gorbachev could not save the country. Some Soviet republics, such as Ukraine and Belarus, declared their independence. Finally, in 1991, the Soviet Union officially came to an end, and Russia became the Russian Federation.

As the Soviet Union crumbled and fell, Russians were excited at the idea of a new Russia. But at the same time, chaos, unrest, and economic troubles continued. With greater freedom to leave if they chose, many people made the same decision as many Russians before them had. Between 1991 and 2005, the fourth—and largest—major wave of Russian immigration brought more than 500,000 former Soviet citizens to the United States. Although it is difficult to pinpoint exactly how many of these people came from Russia and how many came from other republics in the Soviet Union, at least 200,000 are thought to be Russian.

The majority of these recent immigrants are well educated, and many specialize in science or technology. They have put their talents to good use in American laboratories, hospitals, computer companies, and many other fields. Russian American writers, artists, and entertainers still make up a respected community, as well.

*We lived in these apartments until we left for America. There was no heating or plumbing in these apartments, so we had to take care of everything—obtaining fuel, chopping firewood and heating the stove. Every fall, we had to wait on line for two days and two nights to obtain some fuel. We lost all our health there, used it up just to survive.*

*—"Genya," describing life during the last years of the Soviet Union*

As this large new population works to make itself at home in a land thousands of miles from their former country, they face familiar challenges. Just as children of earlier immigrants did—and just as all young Americans do—Russian Americans in modern times have their own conflicts with parents about traditions and change. And for many people, the dramatic difference between Russian life and American life can still cause "culture shock" and leave them feeling overwhelmed or isolated.

But many events, organizations, and traditions help new immigrants make the transition, as well as keeping the established Russian American community strong. Major Russian neighborhoods can still be found in cities such as San Francisco, Los Angeles, Chicago, Detroit, Boston, and New York City. Brighton Beach, New York—where Russian immigrants first settled before World War I—still has one of the country's largest Russian populations. And small towns from Nebraska to Oregon are also home to Russian Americans.

Russian neighborhoods often have synagogues or Orthodox Churches, and religion is still important to many Russian Americans. As a result, holidays remain a great way to bring

*Russian American students at Bookvar Russian Language School in Minneapolis, Minnesota, line up to perform a Russian dance at the school's New Year's celebration in 2005.*

people together and keep old customs alive. Members of the Russian Orthodox Church celebrate major Christian events such as Easter and Christmas, while Russian Jews observe Passover, Hanukkah, and other important Jewish holidays. Many Russian Americans have adopted Thanksgiving. Weddings also tend to be large, festive celebrations. These special occasions, like many Russian American gatherings, almost always feature plenty of delicious food. And thanks to Russian American restaurants, bakeries, and delis, any American with an appetite can enjoy Russian favorites. Shops and markets also offer a variety of Russian goods, from the traditional wooden nesting doll figures called *matryoshkas* to Russian-language magazines and newspapers. And Russians continue to arrive in the United States, adding their own wealth of talents, experiences, and stories to the mix. In addition, more and more American parents have begun adopting orphaned children from Russia, creating a new and growing part of the Russian American community.

With every wave of immigration, Russians have come to the United States filled with hope and determination. They have worked hard to create brighter futures for themselves and their families. Often struggling against great odds, they have overcome many challenges to fulfill their dreams and to become Russian Americans. At the same time, they have brought the history, beauty, culture, and customs of their homeland to their new nation.

# BORSCHT

This hearty beet soup is a common dish in Russia. It has grown into a favorite in the United States as well, and Russian delis and restaurants across the country serve up hot bowls of borscht to hungry customers.

2 RED BEETS

2 CARROTS

1 ONION, PEELED AND HALVED

12 C. BEEF OR VEGETABLE BROTH

3 MEDIUM POTATOES, PEELED

$^1/_4$ HEAD GREEN CABBAGE

1 TBSP. DRIED PARSLEY FLAKES

$^1/_2$ TSP. SALT

1 TSP. LEMON JUICE

$^1/_4$ TSP. BLACK PEPPER

SOUR CREAM AND FRESH DILL TO GARNISH

1. Wash beets and carrots well. Place beets, onion, and one carrot in a large stockpot with 11 c. of the broth. Bring to a boil over high heat. Then reduce heat to medium and use a ladle or large spoon to skim off foam that forms on the surface. Cook for 20 to 25 minutes, or until vegetables are soft.

2. Remove vegetables from pot. Discard onion, and set beet mixture aside to cool.

3. Cut potatoes into quarters. Slice cabbage into strips. Peel and slice raw carrot. Add potatoes, cabbage, raw carrot, parsley, salt, and remaining 1 c. broth to pot. Cook for 30 minutes.

4. Peel cooled beets and cooked carrot. Grate or chop finely, add to soup, and cook 10 to 15 minutes longer.

5. Add lemon juice and pepper. Stir and serve hot, garnishing each bowl with a dollop of sour cream and a small piece of dill.

Serves 6

# FAMOUS RUSSIAN AMERICANS

### RICHARD AVEDON (1923–2004)

Born in New York City, Avedon dropped out of high school as a young man to join the Merchant Marines as a photographer. His next job was taking pictures for a department store, and from there he went on to work for more and more prominent magazines. He eventually emerged as one of the most influential artists of the twentieth century, known for his elegant fashion photography as well as for his creative and moving portraits of politicians, celebrities, and ordinary Americans.

### GEORGE BALANCHINE

(1904–1983) Born in Saint Petersburg, Balanchine began taking piano lessons at the age of five and was a student at the Imperial Theater School by the age of nine. He eventually started to explore choreography (dance arrangement), and—despite the chaos of the Russian Revolution—graduated with honors in 1921. After several years as a dancer, Balanchine came to the United States in 1933, where he changed his name (originally Georgy Melitonovitch Balanchivadze) to something more "American" and helped establish the School of American Ballet and the American Ballet Company. Balanchine is seen as one of the most important choreographers in modern American ballet.

### NINA BERBEROVA (1901–1993)

Berberova, born in Saint Petersburg, began jotting down poems as a girl and dreamed of being a writer. But when she graduated from college in the same year as the Russian Revolution, her plans were shattered. Along with many other artists and intellectuals, she fled Russia in 1922. She moved first to

Germany and then to France, and in 1950 she immigrated to the United States. First working as a clerk while studying English, she went on to become a literature professor and an editor and translator of Russian works, while also continuing to write. She is especially well known for examining the lives of Russians in America.

## IRVING BERLIN (1888–1989)

Born in Russia (though it is unknown exactly where), Berlin moved to New York City with his Russian Jewish family as a small child. His father died when Berlin was only thirteen, and he worked at odd jobs to help support his mother and seven siblings. But before long, Berlin had begun a successful career as a composer. His first song was published in 1907, and he went on to write hundreds of songs—many of them American favorites such as "White Christmas," "God Bless America," and "Easter Parade."

## SERGEY BRIN (b. 1974)

Brin was born in Moscow. When he was five years old, he and his parents came to the United States as part of new programs allowing Jewish emigration. He took an interest in math and computers as a boy and studied these topics at the University of Maryland and at Stanford University in Berkeley, California. When Brin and Larry Page, another Stanford student, were working on a research project, they got the idea for a new kind of Internet tool. In 1998 they founded Google, a popular Internet search engine known for being efficient and easy to use. By 2005 Google was a multibillion-dollar business. But even as a successful U.S. businessperson, Brin has not forgotten Russia or his roots there. He still enjoys favorite foods from his homeland and often dines at Russian restaurants in San Francisco, where he lives.

## JOSEPH BRODSKY (1940–1996)

Born in Leningrad, Brodsky began writing poetry when he was eighteen years old. In 1972 he was exiled by the Soviet government for writing what officials called "partisan" and "decadent" poetry. Taking refuge in the United States, Brodsky went on to become a professor and a poet-in-residence at several prominent American universities, including Columbia University in New York City. He won the Nobel Prize for Literature for his work in 1987, and his books—which include *Selected Poems* and the collection of essays *Less Than One*—have been translated into more than ten languages.

## SERGEI FEDOROV (b. 1969)

Born in Pskov, Russia, Fedorov started skating early in life. Encouraged by his father, who helped him train, Federov became a hockey player and eventually joined the Moscow team. After four years there, he was spotted by the U.S. National Hockey League, and in 1989 he was drafted by the Detroit Red Wings. During his thirteen years with that team, he was recognized as a star player and won several awards for his performance. During that time, the Red Wings won the Stanley Cup— U.S. professional hockey's highest prize—three times. In 2003 he left Detroit and joined the Anaheim Mighty Ducks in California in 2003. Since then he has continued to be recognized as an outstanding player and has also continued to play hockey for Russia, helping the nation win Olympic medals in 1998 and 2002.

## HARRISON FORD (b. 1942)

Born in Chicago, Illinois, to a Russian Jewish mother and an Irish Catholic father, Harrison Ford fell in love with acting as a young man. Picking up and moving to Hollywood from Wisconsin, where he'd been in college, he was able to get small roles in television shows and movies here and there. Then, in

1973, he got his big break when he appeared in the movie *American Graffiti*. He went on to become a full-fledged star as Han Solo in the *Star Wars* trilogy and also as Indiana Jones in a series of movies about an adventurous archaeologist. He continues to make movies, while also enjoying spending time at his ranch in Wyoming.

## ANNA KOURNIKOVA (b. 1981)

Born in Moscow, Anna Kournikova received her first tennis racket as a Christmas gift from her parents when she was five years old and began competing in local tournaments by the age of nine. Soon recognized for her talent and potential, she and her parents moved to Florida when she was eleven years old so that she could receive intensive training. She became a professional player in 1995, soon winning a number of international competitions and staking a claim as one of the world's most popular female tennis players. Although she announced her retirement from professional tennis in 2004, she has also explored other activities such as acting and modeling.

## NATALIA MAKAROVA (b. 1940)

Born to musician parents in Saint Petersburg, Makarova started dancing at the age of thirteen. After six years of training with Saint Petersburg's Kirov Ballet company, she advanced to become a member of the company ballet troupe. But Makarova felt stifled by the artistic limitations imposed by the Soviet government. In 1970, while performing in Great Britain, she left the troupe and defected from the Soviet Union. She moved to the United States and joined the American Ballet Theatre, were she danced many leading roles. She went on to dance as a guest star for ballet companies around the world, found her own ballet company, win a Tony Award for her role in a Broadway play, and appear in television programs. During the more open Gorbachev era, she even danced with the Kirov in Russia again before retiring in 1989.

## YEHUDI MENUHIN (1916–1999)

Born in New York City to Russian Jewish parents who had recently immigrated, the young Menuhin showed great talent as a violinist. At the age of seven, he won widespread attention with an outstanding performance of Mendelssohn's *Violin Concerto*, and he began touring the world as a teenager. During World War II, he played for troops in Europe, and after the war, he performed a special concert for survivors of the Holocaust. In 1963 he founded the Yehudi Menuhin School for musically talented children. He remained a popular violinist, while also branching out into conducting, writing books, and teaching.

## GARY SHTEYNGART (b. 1972)

Shteyngart was born in Saint Petersburg and moved to the United States at the age of nine. He published his first novel, *The Russian Debutante's Handbook*, when he was thirty years old. This story of a Russian immigrant's experiences in America became a great success, earning Shteyngart a number of awards including the Stephen Crane Award for First Fiction. Shteyngart, who lives in New York City, also writes essays and short stories.

## IGOR STRAVINSKY (1882–1971)

Stravinsky was born in Saint Petersburg. When he was not yet twenty years old, his first compositions were produced by the Russian Imperial Ballet. In 1910 he traveled to France, where his first major ballet, *The Firebird*, was produced and choreographed by a fellow Russian, Sergy Diaghilev. In 1913 Stravinsky wrote his masterpiece, *The Rite of Spring*. At its premiere in Paris, the piece caused such strong feelings among its listeners—some who were enthusiastic and others who were upset by its unconventional rhythms and melodies—that it nearly caused a riot. After World War II, Stravinsky left the Soviet Union for the United States, where he continued to compose and conduct until he died in New York in 1971.

## NATALIE WOOD (1938–1981)

Born in San Francisco as Natalia Nikolaevna Zakharenko, Wood was the daughter of Russian Jewish immigrants. She began acting at a young age, appearing in her first movie at the age of four. She eventually took the stage name Natalie Wood, and in 1947 she appeared in the Christmas classic *Miracle on 34th Street*. Her first major role as an adult was in 1955, when she costarred with James Dean in *Rebel without a Cause*. Wood won the role of Maria in the movie version of Leonard Bernstein's *West Side Story* and played the young Gypsy Rose Lee in the film *Gypsy*. Wood died in a drowning accident in 1981.

## VLADIMIR ZWORYKIN

(1889–1982) Born in Murom (about 200 miles east of Moscow), Zworykin graduated from Saint Petersburg's Imperial Institute of Technology in 1912. After World War I, Zworykin came to the United States and worked as a researcher for Westinghouse Electric Corporation and the Radio Corporation of America. Zworykin invented the first iconoscope, a camera tube that made an all-electronic television system possible, and this invention earned him the nickname of the Father of Television. He also did other valuable research and helped develop other electronic inventions. In 1966 he received the National Medal of Science for his work, and in 1977 he was elected to the National Inventors Hall of Fame. Outside of his work, he enjoyed hobbies such as music and art.

# TIMELINE

| | |
|---|---|
| **late 800s** | Prince Oleg founds Kievan Rus. |
| **1200s** | Mongol invaders take control of Russian lands. |
| **1533** | Ivan the Terrible becomes czar of Russia. |
| **1600s** | The Molokans leave the Russian Orthodox Church. |
| **1724** | Czar Peter the Great orders an expedition to Siberia's far eastern coast, seeking a land route to North America. |
| **1741** | Vitus Bering reaches North America, landing in the Aleutian Islands. |
| **late 1700s** | Mennonites move to Russia. |
| **1791** | A new law limits Jewish residence and travel to the Pale of Settlement. |
| **1861** | Czar Alexander II abolishes serfdom. |
| **1880s** | The first major wave of Russian immigration begins. |
| **late 1800s** | Pogroms against Russian Jews begin sweeping through the Russian countryside. |
| **1892** | Ellis Island Immigration Station opens to handle the many immigrants arriving in the United States. |
| **1913** | Igor Stravinsky's *The Rite of Spring* is performed for the first time. |
| **1914** | World War I begins. |
| **1917** | The Russian Revolution takes place. |
| **1919–1920** | The Red Scare begins. Thousands of Russians in America are arrested. |

| 1922 | The Union of Soviet Socialist Republics (often called the Soviet Union) is formed. |
|------|-----------------------------------------------------------------------------------|
| 1927 | Stalin takes power. |
| 1939 | World War II begins. |
| 1945 | World War II ends, sparking the third major wave of Russian immigration. The Cold War begins. |
| 1950s | Senator Joseph McCarthy seeks to remove suspected Communists from the U.S. government. Russian Americans face hostility and discrimination due to a wave of strong anti-Communism. |
| 1960s | The fourth wave of Russian immigration begins slowly as more people leave the Soviet Union. |
| 1974 | Writer Alexander Solzhenitsyn is exiled by the Soviet government. |
| 1975 | Restrictions on Jewish emigration from the Soviet Union are loosened. |
| 1987 | Russian American poet Joseph Brodsky wins the Nobel Prize for Literature. |
| 1991 | The Soviet Union crumbles. |
| 1992 | The Russian Federation is formed. |
| 1998 | Sergy Brin and Larry Page found Google. |
| 2004 | Sergei Fedorov becomes the first Russian-born hockey player in the United States to reach one thousand points (through goals or assists). |

# GLOSSARY

**ANTI-SEMITISM:** strong hostility or prejudice against Jewish people. Anti-Semitism in Russia and the Soviet Union drove many Russian Jews to leave for other countries, including the United States.

**COLD WAR:** competition and hostility between the United States and the Soviet Union after World War II. During the Cold War, many Americans were strongly anti-Communist, leading some to be prejudiced against Russian Americans.

**COMMUNISM:** a political and economic system. In a Communist country, the government controls business, farming, and trade.

**CZAR:** an all-powerful emperor of Russia

**DEFECTOR:** a person who leaves his or her country for political reasons, usually without the government's permission. Many people defected from the Soviet Union to find greater freedom in the United States or other countries.

**EXILE:** to force a person to leave his or her home. The Soviet Union exiled many Russians for their activities and beliefs.

**GULAG:** a hard-labor camp. Under Stalin, millions of Russians were imprisoned in Siberian gulags.

**IMMIGRATE:** to come to live in a country other than one's homeland. A person who immigrates is called an immigrant.

**POGROMS:** organized and sometimes government-approved attacks on Jews. Pogroms took place in Russia in the late 1800s and early 1900s.

**RED SCARE:** a period of intense paranoia about Communism in the United States. The Red Scare took place after the Russian Revolution and resulted in prejudice against Russian immigrants.

**SERFS:** peasants, or farmworkers, forced to live and work on the property of wealthy landowners. Serfs were fed and housed in return for their labor, but they were considered the property of the landowners and their rights were very limited.

web enhanced at **www.inamericabooks.com**

# THINGS TO SEE AND DO

BRIGHTON BEACH
BROOKLYN, NEW YORK
http://www.brightonbeach.com/
As one of the largest Russian American communities in the country, Brighton Beach offers plenty of sights and activities. Russian groceries, restaurants, and shops line the neighborhood's main street, and the boardwalk along the water is a favorite place to stroll. Cultural events include the annual Brighton Jubilee, which features food, live entertainment, rides, and other activities and draws more than 100,000 guests every summer.

ELLIS ISLAND IMMIGRATION MUSEUM
NEW YORK, NEW YORK
http://www.ellisisland.com
Visit the immigration museum on Ellis Island to walk in the footsteps of Russian immigrants to America. Step off a ferry onto the dock where new arrivals from Russia disembarked. Stroll through the station's Great Hall, view exhibits of personal belongings, and look for the names of your relatives in the list of immigrants who passed through the station.

FORT ROSS STATE HISTORIC PARK
JENNER, CALIFORNIA
http://www.parks.ca.gov/
?page_id=449
Founded in 1812 by Russian explorers and promyshlenniki, Fort Ross was a trading post for nearly thirty years and was one of the earliest Russian settlements in America. Some of the site's historic structures have been rebuilt, and visitors can see sights such as a Russian Orthodox chapel and an exhibit of historical artifacts.

RUSSIAN AMERICAN KIDS CIRCUS
BROOKLYN, NEW YORK
http://www.rakidscircus.org/index1.htm
Established in 1994 by Alex Berenchtein, this performance troupe features Russian American boys and girls, from six to sixteen years old, doing breathtaking stunts, including tightrope-walking, acrobatics, juggling, and more.

RUSSIAN CENTER
SAN FRANCISCO, CALIFORNIA
http://www.russiancentersf.com/
This community center, which dates back to 1939, hosts a variety of

Russian American events, from classes on folk dancing to the annual Russian Festival, featuring live music, art exhibits, and plenty of food. The center is also home to the Museum of Russian Culture, the offices of the *Russian Life Daily Newspaper*, and a library of Russian literature for children and adults.

SITKA, ALASKA
http://www.sitka.org

This city—established in 1799 as New Archangel—is home to a wealth of Russian American history. See the New Archangel Dancers perform traditional Russian numbers, visit the Russian Orthodox Saint Michael the Archangel Cathedral or the Russian cemetery, stop by the Isabel Miller Museum to see historical photographs and displays, and explore buildings dating back to the early 1800s.

# SOURCE NOTES

12   Alexander Pushkin, trans. Charles Johnston, *Eugene Onegin and Other Poems* (New York: Alfred A. Knopf, 1999), 35.

13   Stanford Neil Gerber, *Russkaya Celo: The Ethnography of a Russian-American Community* (New York: AMS Press, 1985), 15.

15   Warren B. Walsh, ed., *Readings in Russian History* (Syracuse, NY: Syracuse University Press, 1950), 284.

18   Mary Antin, *The Promised Land*, n.d., http://digital.library .upenn.edu/women/antin/ land/land.html (February 9, 2005).

21   Ibid.

24   Gerber, *Russkaya Celo*, 26.

25   John Glad, *Russia Abroad: Writers, History, Politics* (Tenafly, NJ: Hermitage and Birchbark, 1999), 98.

31   Jerome Davis, *The Russian Immigrant* (New York: Arno Press, 1969), 76.

34  Susan Wiley Hardwick, *Russian Refuge: Religion, Migration, and Settlement on the North American Pacific Rim* (Chicago: University of Chicago Press, 1993), 102.

37  Gerber, *Russkaya Celo*, 39.

42  Alex Shoumatoff, *Russian Blood: A Family Chronicle* (New York: Vintage Books, 1990), 111.

44  Davis, *The Russian Immigrant*, 24–25.

47  Vera Kishinevsky, *Russian Immigrants in the United States: Adapting to American Culture* (New York: LFB Scholarly Publishing, 2004), 26.

51  Robert S. Jaster, *Russian Voices on the Kennebec: The Story of Maine's Unlikely Colony* (Orono: The University of Maine Press, 1999), 79.

57  Kishinevsky, *Russian Immigrants in the United States*, 28.

59  Ibid., 45.

# SELECTED BIBLIOGRAPHY

Davis, Jerome. *The Russian Immigrant*. New York: Arno Press, 1969. This book provides a wealth of statistics and detailed information about Russian immigrants in the early twentieth century. Living conditions, social customs, and other topics are discussed.

Davis Center for Russian and Eurasian Studies at Harvard. "Russia, the Former Soviet Republics, and Eastern Europe." N.d. http://www.fas.harvard.edu/~gstudies/russia/russcurriculum.htm (January 26, 2005). This site provides an overview of the history of Russian immigration to the United States.

Department of Homeland Security: Office of Immigration Statistics. "2003 Yearbook of Immigration Statistics." September 2004. http://uscis.gov/graphics/shared/aboutus/statistics/2003Yearbook.pdf

(January 26, 2005). This document provides detailed statistics on recent immigration, as well as helpful historical information.

Gerber, Stanford Neil. *Russkaya Celo: The Ethnography of a Russian-American Community.* New York: AMS Press, 1985. This detailed study examines an unnamed Russian American town in the Midwestern United States. Numerous interviews with immigrants themselves offer insight into their thoughts and feelings about Russia, America, and their lives.

Glad, John. *Russia Abroad: Writers, History, Politics.* Tenafly, NJ: Hermitage and Birchbark, 1999. This book takes a look at the reasons for and results of Russian emigration to both the United States and beyond.

Hardwick, Susan Wiley. *Russian Refuge: Religion, Migration, and Settlement on the North American Pacific Rim.* Chicago: University of Chicago Press, 1993. Focusing on immigration to the western United States and Canada, this book includes interviews and discussion about Russian American communities, adaptation to American life, religion, and other topics.

Kishinevsky, Vera. *Russian Immigrants in the United States: Adapting to American Culture.* New York: LFB Scholarly Publishing, 2004. This book examines the experience of Russian American women. Each case study focuses on three generations of a Russian immigrant family: grandmother, mother, and daughter.

# FURTHER READING & WEBSITES

## NONFICTION

Daniels, Roger. *American Immigration: A Student Companion.* New York: Oxford University Press,

2001. This encyclopedia of immigration facts, figures, and terms offers a helpful overview of immigration to the United States, from legal issues to

personal stories. Maps, photographs, and other materials also add depth to the text.

Hoobler, Dorothy, and Thomas Hoobler. *The Jewish American Family Album.* New York: Oxford University Press, 1995. Letters, diaries, and photographs tell the story of Jewish immigration to the United States from Russia and other countries.

Kristy, Davida. *George Balanchine: American Ballet Master.* Minneapolis: Lerner Publications Company, 1996. This biography takes a look at the life of a famous Russian American and his contributions to ballet in the United States.

Lawlor, Veronica, ed. *I Was Dreaming to Come to America: Memories from the Ellis Island Oral History Project.* New York: Viking, 1995. This illustrated book presents first-person memories of immigrant children. Although quite short, the book is interesting and informative.

Márquez, Herón. *Russia in Pictures.* Minneapolis: Lerner Publications Company, 2004. This book introduces readers to the land, history, and culture of Russia.

Plotkin, Gregory, and Rita Plotkin. *Cooking the Russian Way.* Minneapolis: Lerner Publications Company, 2003. This cultural cookbook presents recipes for authentic and traditional Russian dishes, including information about and recipes related to holidays and festivals.

Sherman, Josepha. *The Cold War.* Minneapolis: Lerner Publications Company, 2004. This title provides background information on the Cold War, which affected relationships between Russian Americans and their neighbors between 1945 and the early 1990s.

Stein, R. Conrad. *The Great Red Scare.* Parsippany, NJ: New Discovery Books, 1998. This book investigates the events of the second Red Scare, which took place during the Cold War and affected many Russian Americans.

Streissguth, Tom. *Say It with Music: A Story about Irving Berlin.* Minneapolis: Carolrhoda Books, Inc., 1994. This book explores the life and career of Irving Berlin, one of America's most beloved songwriters.

Zamenova, Tatyana. *Teenage Refugees from Russia Speak Out.* New York: Rosen Publishing Group, 1995. In personal interviews, young Russian Americans talk about what it is like to leave home and start over.

# FICTION

Avery, Gillian. *Russian Fairy Tales.* New York: Knopf, 1995. This collection of classic Russian stories is a good introduction to the country's traditional folkore.

Lasky, Kathryn. *Dreams in the Golden Country: The Diary of Zipporah Feldman, a Jewish Immigrant Girl.* New York: Scholastic, 1998. When Zipporah and her family flee Russia to escape anti-Semitism and persecution, they are excited to start their new lives. But, settling in the Lower East Side in New York City, they find that immigrant life presents many challenges of its own.

Sherman, Eileen Bluestone. *Independence Avenue.* Philadelphia: Jewish Publication Society, 1990. Elias Cherevnosky, a Russian Jew, immigrates to the United States in the early 1900s when he is fourteen years old. As he struggles to overcome the challenges of adjusting to his new home, he misses his family in Russia but also discovers many joys of life in the United States.

# WEBSITES

THE FACE OF RUSSIA
http://www.pbs.org/weta/faceofrussia/
This site from PBS presents an overview of major events and figures in Russian history.

IMMIGRATION: POLISH/RUSSIAN
http://memory.loc.gov/learn/features/immig/polish.html
This Library of Congress website explores the history of immigration to the United States from both Russia and Poland, discussing Soviet exiles, the Jewish immigrant community in New York's Lower East Side, and more.

**INAMERICABOOKS.COM**
http://www.inamericabooks.com
Visit inamericabooks.com, the
online home of the In America
series, to get linked to all sorts of
useful information. You'll find
historical and cultural websites
related to individual groups, as
well as general information on
genealogy, creating your own
family tree, and the history of
immigration in America.

**RED FILES**
http://www.pbs.org/redfiles/
This website explores Russia's
Soviet era, from the KGB—secret
police that terrorized many
Russians—to the competition
between the United States and
the Soviet Union in sports, space
exploration, and more.

# INDEX

Alaska, 10–11, 35
Alexander II (czar), 12, 68
Avedon, Richard, 62

Balanchine, George, 62
Berberova, Nina, 62–63
Berlin, Irving, 63
Brin, Sergey, 63
Brodsky, Joseph, 55, 64

Catherine the Great (czarina,) 16, 36
Chicago, Illinois, 28, 29, 58, 64
children, 4, 15, 19, 23, 24, 25, 34–35, 36, 37–38, 47, 59, 66
Cold War, 52–54, 56, 69
Communism, 39, 40, 41–42, 52, 54, 56, 45, 69; Red Scare, 44–47, 52. *See also* Communist Party; Lenin, Vladimir Ilich; McCarthy, Joseph; Stalin, Joseph; Union of Soviet Socialist Republics
Communist Party, 40, 45, 47; Bolsheviks, 40, 41, 44. *See also* Communism
customs and traditions, 5, 18–19, 32, 33, 34–37, 44, 52, 58–59, 72
czar, 7, 8, 9, 10, 12, 14–15, 18–19, 38–39, 43, 47, 68, 70. *See also* Alexander II (czar); Ivan IV (Ivan the Terrible) (czar); Peter the Great (czar)
czarist Russia, 8–9,  41; life in, 9, 12–15; escape from, 15, 16–18, 18–19, 20–21

deportation, 44
diet (nutrition), 10, 11, 13, 15, 21, 25, 31, 38, 42, 49, 56, 59, 71, 72. *See also* recipe: borscht
discrimination and persecution, 54, 69; anti–Semitism, 18–19, 20, 21, 68; gulags (Russian prisons),

47–48, 55, 70; Pale of Settlement, 18, 19, 68; pogroms, 19, 68, 70; Red Scare, 44–47, 52. *See also* refugees; religion

employment and businesses, 10–11, 12–14, 19, 22–29, 32–33, 63, 70, 44, 46, 51–52; Alaskan venture, the, 10–11
exile, 15, 18, 55, 64, 69, 70–71

farming, 6, 9, 12, 13, 15, 16, 24, 30, 32–33, 36, 70
Fedorov, Sergei, 64, 69
Ford, Harrison, 64–65

Gorbachev, Mikhail, 57, 65

health and medicine, 15, 21, 23, 25, 28, 31, 35–36, 57
holidays and festivals, 58–59, 72
housing, 4, 12, 13, 14–15, 29–31, 33, 38, 70

immigrant(s) and immigration, 2, 15, 16–18, 19, 24, 27, 28, 29–31, 32–33, 34–38, 44–46, 51, 58, 59, 63, 66, 67, 68, 69, 70; Ellis Island, 19, 22–23, 71; major waves of, 4, 5, 20–21, 42–43, 51–52, 57, 58, 59, 68, 69
Ivan IV (Ivan the Terrible), czar, 8–9, 68

Kievan Rus, 6, 66
Kournikova, Anna, 65

labor: strikes, 28–29; sweatshops, 25; unions, 15, 27–29, 45; wages, 13, 15, 24, 27, 29; working conditions, 13, 25, 26–29, 31. *See also* employment and businesses

**web enhanced at www.inamericabooks.com**

Lenin, Vladimir Ilich, 40, 41, 46

Makarova, Natalia, 54, 65
map, 7
McCarthy, Joseph, 54. *See also*
    Communism
Menuhin, Yehudi, 66
Moscow (Russia), 6, 8, 12, 41, 42, 63,
    64, 65, 67
Museum of Russian Culture, 72

New York City, 22–23, 25, 29, 30, 58,
    62, 63, 64, 66, 71
Nicholas II (czar), 14, 38
Nureyev, Rudolf, 54

Oleg (prince), 6, 68

Peter the Great (czar), 7, 10, 68
Philadelphia, Pennsylvania, 29
poverty, 4, 5, 12, 14, 16, 20, 21, 27, 34,
    35, 38–39, 41

recipe: borscht, 60–61
refugees, 5, 47–52. *See also*
    discrimination and persecution;
    exile
religion, 7, 16–17, 34, 54, 58: Jewish,
    18–19, 20, 25, 28–29, 34–37, 46,
    48, 54, 59, 63, 64, 66, 67, 70;
    Mennonite, 5, 16–18, 32–33, 38,
    68; Molokan, 17–18, 33, 38, 68;
    Roman Catholic, 17; Russian
    Orthodox, 11, 16, 17, 18, 34, 35,
    36–37, 58, 59, 68, 71, 72
Russian Empire. *See* czarist Russia
Russian Federation, 57, 69
Russian Jews. *See* religion: Jewish
Russian neighborhoods, 29–31, 33,
    34, 35, 38, 52, 58–59; Brighton
    Beach (New York City), 58, 71;
    Lower East Side (New York City),
    29
Russian Revolution, 5, 38–39, 40,
    41–43, 44, 46, 48, 62, 68, 70

San Francisco, California, 71–72
Shteyngart, Gary, 66
Siberia, 8, 10, 15, 48, 55, 68, 70
Solzhenitsyn, Alexander, 55, 69
space race, 53
Stalin, Joseph, 5, 47–48, 49, 50, 52, 54,
    68, 70
Stravinsky, Igor, 66, 68

Union of Soviet Socialist Republics
    (Soviet Union), 5, 47, 48–54,
    56–57, 64, 65, 66, 69, 70; collapse
    of, 5, 56–57, 69; life in, 41–43,
    47–52, 54, 56–57

women, 25, 49, 50
Wood, Natalie, 67
World War I, 38, 40, 42, 46, 67, 68
World War II, 5, 48–51, 52, 58, 66, 69,
    70

Zworykin, Vladimir, 67

ACKNOWLEDGMENTS: THE PHOTOGRAPHS IN THIS BOOK ARE REPRODUCED WITH THE PERMISSION OF: © Digital Vision Royalty Free, pp. 1, 3, 22; © Sam Lund/Independent Picture Service, p. 6; Bill Hauser, p. 7; Library of Congress, pp. 9, 11 bottom (HABS, AK, SITKA, 1–27) and inset (LC–USZ62–133017), 23, 32, 35 (HABS, AK, SITKA, 1–28), 36 (LC–DIG–nclc–00363), 66 (right); © Illustrated London News, p. 14; Harry J. Lerner/Independent Picture Service, p. 19; National Archives, p. 20; © California Museum of Photography, Keystone–Mast Collection, University of California, Riverside, p. 26; © Bettmann/CORBIS, pp. 28, 53 (right), 65 (right); © Getty Images, p. 29; © The Art Archive, p. 41; © Brown Brothers, p. 43; © Topical Press Agency/Getty Images, p. 45; © Max Alpert/Slava Katamidze Collection/Getty Images, p. 49; © Ralph Morse/Keystone/Getty Images, p. 50; © Underwood & Underwood/CORBIS, p. 48; © NASA, p. 53 (left); © The Nobel Foundation, p. 55; © Steve Feinstein, p. 56; © Brian Lenk, p. 58; © Walter and Lousieann Pietrowicz/ September 8th Stock, p. 60; © Les Stone/ZUMA Press, p. 62 (top left); © Ballet Society, Inc., p. 62 (bottom left); © Sophie Bassouls/CORBIS, p. 62 (bottom right); Independent Picture Service, p. 63 (left); © Kim Kulish/CORBIS, p. 63 (right); © Reuters/CORBIS, p. 64 (top left); © Shelly Castellano/ZUMA Press, p. 64 (bottom left); © Hollywood Book & Poster, p. 64 (right); © Thomas B. Shea/Icon SMI/ZUMA Press, p. 65 (left); © Angel  Records, p. 66 (left); © Creative Management Associates, p. 67 (top); RCA Corporation, p. 67 (bottom).

Front Cover: © Independent Picture Service; © Digital Vision Royalty Free (title); © Sam Lund/Independent Picture Service (bottom). Back Cover: © Digital Vision Royalty Free.